AND NOBODY GOT HURT **2!**

AND NOBODY GOT HURT 2!

The World's
Weirdest, Wackiest,
and Most Amazing
True
^ Sports Stories

LEN BERMAN

Illustrated by Kent Gamble

LITTLE, BROWN AND COMPANY

New York ⟞ Boston

Little, Brown and Company

Hachette Book Group USA
237 Park Avenue, New York, NY 10169
Visit our Web site at www.lb-kids.com

First Edition: October 2007

ISBN-13: 978-0-316-06706-5 (hc)   ISBN-10: 0-316-06706-7 (hc)
ISBN-13: 0-316-06705-8 (pb) ISBN-10: 316-06705-9 (pb)

HC: 10 9 8 7 6 5 4 3 2 1
PB: 10 9 8 7 6 5 4 3 2 1

WOR

Printed in the United States of America

CONTENTS

Pregame Show

So, how's it going? The last time we talked, we made a little deal. If you kept enjoying sports, I'd keep collecting crazy sports stories. Well, I kept my end of the bargain and I'm guessing you did, too. So we meet again. Wait until you read some of the new stuff that's happened in sports.

For example, baseball is so simple. You run to first, second, third, and then home. Fair enough. But when is a home run a single? Even a grand-slam homer? You've heard of a ground rule double, but how about an automatic triple? Rules, rules, rules. The goal line is a very easy place to understand in football. So why do so many players have trouble with it? You're about to find out.

And in golf the idea is straightforward. Just hit the ball. But what if it's underwater? You won't believe what one pro golfer did. Athletes do all sorts of amazing things. One high school kid hit the most incredible basket while lying on his back. It happened in a championship game.

Did you know they have world championships in just about everything? Sure, they have them in the major sports, but did you ever hear of the World Toe Wrestling Championships?

And what's the deal with animals? They're all over the place. There was a pig delay in a baseball game. What was a pig doing on the baseball field? And in horse racing all kinds of weird things have happened. I've seen horse races with dogs, birds, and even earthquakes right in the middle of the race.

Soccer may be the most widely played sport in the world. Again, rather simple. Just use your feet or head to score a goal. But when you read the soccer chapter, you'll find out what chickens, fire-crackers, and pizza all have to do with the sport of soccer.

And I've added a whole new chapter this time around: The Olympics. The entire world gathers in the name of sport. So why is there so much cheating? And if they're the greatest athletes in the world, why do they goof up so much?

So here we go again. And remember my basic rule: "and nobody got hurt." Okay, it's not exactly true all the time. There are a few bumps and bruises along the way. But I promise you won't get hurt reading this book unless you find yourself laughing too hard. So try to control yourself, and at the same time I hope you enjoy my latest collection of the world's weirdest, wackiest, and, this time, most amazing, true sports stories.

BASEBALL

Ah, baseball, the National Pastime. Although, I've got a couple of other ways to describe it. Some call it the only sport where you don't use a clock. Not true! How about golf and tennis? Or cricket, where a game can take several days! Here's another one I like: baseball is the only sport where, when you're on offense, the other team has the ball. Maybe that's why so many weird things seem to happen in baseball.

Another reason may be the dimensions of the ballparks. They're all different. In basketball, football, and hockey the court and the field have standard shapes. Not in baseball. They've got all sorts of nooks and crannies in the outfield and foul territory. That could explain things. In some ballparks the relief pitchers warm up behind the outfield fence. In others they warm up in foul territory. Did you ever see a fielder try to catch a pop-up in foul territory and then trip over the pitcher's mound, where the relievers warm up? Pretty funny, huh? Not for the player who falls.

And without a clock, I've seen some strange delays of game. Not just rain, but bees. I've even seen a pig delay!

How about gloves? Weird stuff happens with them. Players throw gloves at balls that are in play. Is that allowed? I've seen balls bounce off gloves and heads with all sorts of interesting results. How about a World Series decided by a ball bouncing off a shortstop's head?

And things always seem to happen in threes. I'll tell you about some triple plays. Then there's the time three home runs were hit on three consecutive pitches. Hey, that's baseball. Three strikes you're out. Three outs to an inning. Lots of threes. So batter up for my baseball stories. one, two, three go!

Three-in-one

Let's start with three plays in one. How can a batter get a single, a home run, and be called out all on the same play? It happened in April 2006 in Baltimore. With Miguel Tejada on first, Javy Lopez of the Baltimore Orioles hit a home run to left field. Los Angeles Angels left fielder Darin Erstad leaped at the wall to catch it, but he fell down with his glove empty and the ball in the stands. Tejada was running around the bases, but he thought the ball had been caught. So he started to run back to first base. While he was doing that, Lopez passed him in the base path. That's a no-no. Lopez was immediately called out, and Tejada was allowed to score since it was really a home run. However, Lopez was credited with a single. So there you have it. Lopez hit a homer, got credited with a single, and was called out, all on the same play!

Not-so-grand-slam

During the 1999 National League Playoffs at Shea Stadium, the New York Mets were facing elimination at the hands of the Atlanta Braves in game five. It went to the bottom of the fifteenth inning, and the game was tied 3–3. The Mets had the bases loaded when Robin Ventura hit a grand-slam homer to win the game. His teammates ran onto the field to mob him, and Ventura never made it to second base. Since he didn't round the bases, Ventura's hit was ruled a single. So while the final score should have been 7–3, it goes into the record books as a 4–3 final thanks to Robin Ventura's "grand-slam single"!

1–2–3

In Oakland in April 2006, the Oakland A's put on an impressive hitting display. Eric Chavez led off the bottom of the sixth inning. On the first pitch from Texas Ranger Vicente Padilla, Chavez hit a home run. The next batter was Frank Thomas. The first pitch to him . . . another home run. The next batter was Milton Bradley. The first pitch to him . . . ditto! Three consecutive pitches resulted in three home runs. Joaquín Benoit relieved Padilla. The next batter was Marco Scutaro. Alas, he could not make it four for four. A simple groundout.

Pretty in pink

Major league baseball teams do all kinds of things to torment their rookies. It's a tradition. For example, the rookies might be forced to wear women's clothing to go on a road trip. One time the New York Yankees rookies were forced to dress

up as female cheerleaders, with short skirts and pom-poms. In April 2004, Philadelphia Phillies relief pitcher Ryan Wagner headed down to the bull pen before the game with the rest of the Phillies relievers. Wagner had to wear a Barbie backpack as his rookie initiation. It was pretty and pink. And

Wagner, in his full baseball uniform, proudly walked from the dugout all the way out to the bullpen wearing his pretty pink Barbie backpack.

Here's something else they did to a rookie. In May 2004 at Fenway Park, Boston, Red Sox rookie Kevin Youkilis hit his first major league home run. As he returned to the dugout, instead of congratulating him, his teammates totally ignored him. So he proceeded to "high-five" his imaginary teammates. He went around the dugout slapping high fives into thin air.

Money to burn

In April 2004, a minor league team in Michigan came up with a unique promotion. The Battle Creek Yankees decided to pay fans to show up. What a deal. Not only did fans get a free ticket to the game but they were also given a free dollar bill. Now you have to know that an April night in Michigan is not exactly a picnic. It was cold that night. But the promotion paid off (I think). Attendance *zoomed* that night from an average of 515 fans all the way up to 660!

Here's another one. How would you like to spend the night at the ballpark? In May 2004 on

Mother's Day, there was a unique promotion at the St. Paul Saints game in Minnesota. Game time: 5:30 a.m. Fans were allowed to pitch tents and camp out on the field all night long. They were awakened in time to watch the game. I'm told some fans had a "nutritious" breakfast of Krispy Kreme doughnuts and beer!

Delay of game

I've heard of all sorts of reasons why baseball games get delayed. Rain, snow, fog, too many gnats. You name it, it's happened. The lights went out, or the umpires didn't show up. But how about this one? In May 2004 at a minor league game in Indianapolis, the inning was about to begin, but they couldn't find the first baseman. All the other fielders were in place, but Jeff Lieber was nowhere to be found. Turns out he went to the bathroom between innings and locked himself in. He finally made it out, but the game was delayed several minutes. Lieber later said he hoped that when his baseball career was over he wouldn't be remembered as "the guy who got stuck in the john." Here's another one. In March 2005, in an exhibition game in Tucson between Colorado and

Arizona, there was a "bee delay." A swarm of bees attacked the field. In fact, that game was not only delayed, but it also had to be called off before the sixth inning began. Why did the bees attack? They were attracted to Colorado pitcher Darren Oliver. He had coconut oil in his hair gel and it drove the bees wild. Said Oliver, "I guess I smelled good."

How about a pig delay? In a Mexican league baseball game in December 2005, a pig got loose on

the field in the middle of the game. Players started chasing it in the outfield. The clever pig then started running toward the infield with players and groundskeepers running in hot pursuit of it. The elusive little fellow ran from left field to the shortstop, to near home plate, and then took off running toward right field. One of those chasing the pig was the chicken mascot. As the pig approached the baseline area between first and second, the mascot took off his head and threw it, hitting the pig. The little guy was stopped in his tracks and the mascot was then able to tackle him. Nobody got hurt, but it brought up an interesting rule. What would have happened if the pig had swallowed a baseball that was still in play? After scouring the rule book I found the ruling: an inside the *pork* home run! (Ha-ha.)

*Get out your **real** rule book*

In May 2005, Los Angeles Dodgers pitcher Duaner Sanchez was on the mound. The batter hit the ball over Sanchez's head, so he just threw his glove up in the air and hit the ball. In baseball, that's not allowed. Do you know the rule if a player throws his glove and hits a batted ball in play? It's an automatic triple for the batter. *Who needs a glove anyway?*

In August 2005 in San Diego, New York Mets third baseman David Wright didn't need his glove at all. In the seventh inning, Brian Giles of the Padres hit a short bloop into left field. Wright ran with his back to home plate, extended his bare right hand, and caught the ball before falling to the ground. Even the hometown fans gave Wright a big ovation. It recalled another bare-handed catch by Kevin Mitchell of the Giants in 1989. Ozzie Smith hit it for St. Louis, and Mitchell, who was playing left field, ran into foul territory. With his back to the plate, Mitchell simply reached up and plucked the fly ball out of the air with his bare hand. So give David Wright and Kevin Mitchell a hand: they certainly don't need a glove!

Hey, that's my ball!

In a baseball game in Colorado in May 2004, the Rockies were hosting the Atlanta Braves. There was a high pop-up near the third-base stands, and Rockies third baseman Vinny

Castilla reached into the crowd to make the catch. He caught it cleanly in his glove and you could see the ball in the top part of his mitt, what the announcers call "an ice cream cone catch." He held onto the ball for a couple of seconds and then a fan just reached into his glove and took the ball out. The umpire ruled that it wasn't a catch! The manager of the Rockies, Clint Hurdle, argued with the umps and got himself thrown out of the game. And the fan who stole the ball was a Rockies fan!

Give that ball a hand

In September 2004 in Atlanta, the Braves were hosting the Phillies. In the fourth inning, the Braves' Charles Thomas hit a fly ball to deep center field. The Philadelphia center fielder Jason Michaels raced back and got his glove on the ball, but didn't catch it. It bounced up into the air again. So one more time he swiped his glove at the ball and this time he hit the ball over the fence with his glove. So what's the rule? Well, the ball never touched the field or the wall, so it counted as a home run! Usually it's a bat that hits the ball out

of the park, not a glove.
Follow the bouncing ball

At least with the Jason Michaels play, there was
no chance of anything getting hurt except for
Michaels's ego. The previous September in
Cleveland, the Indians' Jhonny Peralta hit a fly ball
to right field. It was a bright day and the
Minnesota right fielder Michael Ryan lost the ball
in the sun. At the last second he turned away and
the ball hit him squarely on top of his head.
Fortunately for the Twins, the center fielder
Dustan Mohr came over to "back up" the play.
The ball bounced directly off Ryan's head and into
Mohr's glove for an out. And nobody got hurt!

Speaking of weird bounces, I've never seen a
ground ball quite like this one at Fenway Park in
Boston in August 2004. Julio Lugo was batting for
Tampa Bay and he squibbed a ball foul outside the
first base line. The ball stayed very foul for a while
and then took a big left-hand turn and rolled into
fair territory. The first baseman for Boston, Doug
Mientkiewicz, bent down to field the ball and, just
as he did, the ball hit the first base bag and bounced
away toward second. Even though the ball had first

rolled foul, if it then rolls fair it's a fair ball. The entire time this was happening, Lugo was standing at home plate just watching. When he saw the ball hit the base, he decided, "Gee, maybe it's time to run." He did. And he made it safely to first!

Heads up!

In June 2005 at Dodger Stadium in Los Angeles, Jason Phillips was the batter for the Dodgers. He popped the ball into short right field and Milwaukee second baseman Bill Hall made a terrific catch by the foul line. When he caught it, Jayson Werth of the Dodgers tagged up at third base and tried to score. At that very moment, Phillips was walking off the field in foul territory, heading back to the dugout. Hall threw to the plate but by mistake he nailed Phillips right in the head, the ball smacking off of his batting helmet. Phillips fell to the ground. Imagine that. You hit the ball and somehow during the same play the ball hits you! The result of all this? Werth scored from third, Hall was charged with an error, and nobody got hurt! Phillips stayed in the game,

which Milwaukee wound up winning 7–5.

Now here's one of the wildest shots to the head in baseball history. It happened in the Caribbean World Series in February 2006 in Venezuela. Venezuela was playing against the favored Dominican Republic. In the ninth inning, Venezuela was close to winning the series. With a runner on first and one out, Henry Blanco for Venezuela hit a high pop-up to short left field. Shortstop Erick Aybar went out to make the catch for the Dominican Republic. At the last moment, he turned his back toward home plate, thinking the left fielder Napoleon Calzado would make the catch. The ball came down and hit Aybar right on top of the head. It then rolled away toward left field. The series-clinching run came around to score as bedlam erupted. Fireworks exploded. Venezuela had scored two runs in the bottom of the ninth inning to win the series. It was the first time Venezuela had won the Caribbean World Series in seventeen years. All because of a "hit in the head."

Look out below!

Challenger is a bald eagle who is trained to fly

in baseball stadiums at the end of the playing of the National Anthem. When the song ends, he comes swooping in from the outfield to land on the arm of his trainer, who is standing on the pitcher's mound. Well, in October 2003, the New York Yankees were about to open a playoff series with their archrivals, the Boston Red Sox, at Yankee Stadium. That night, Challenger had a most interesting flight. Just as he was swooping toward the pitcher's mound, a couple of F-14 fighter planes roared over Yankee Stadium in a "flyby." It was part of the pregame ceremony. All of the Yankee players were lined up along the first-base line. Challenger got spooked by the noise of the planes and immediately dived toward the ground, nearly hitting Yankee stars Derek Jeter and Jason Giambi in the head. If the two of them hadn't ducked at the last moment, they might have been injured by a bald eagle. Wouldn't that have been one of the weirdest injuries in sports history?

A rooster booster

Did you hear the one about the rooster who got thrown out of the baseball game? A rooster by the name of Cocky-Doodle-Lou was the mascot for the University of South Carolina baseball team. He would perch himself on top of the first base dugout. But in March 2004 some fans claimed that the rooster smelled, and that he dropped his feathers all over the place. They banned him from the games except for once a week. One fan claimed that he didn't smell anything. Another said, "We're discriminating against the little guy." Before Cocky-Doodle-Lou was banished, the baseball team was 17–0. Afterwards, they lost four of their next eight games. Hmmm.

A *hairy situation*

At the Potomac Nationals minor league baseball game in August 2005, they staged the "Hairiest Back at the Ballpark" contest. Contestants took off their shirts and judges decided who had the hairiest back. Forty-seven-year-old Jim Coffey of Fairfax, Virginia, is basically bald on top, but not on his back. He was declared the winner. His prize? Free laser hair-removal!

Baseball

Hitting the cutoff man

When you play defense in baseball, the cutoff man is important. If a ball is hit into the outfield, and if the throw is going to be made home to try to catch a runner, one of the infielders goes roughly halfway between the outfielder and home plate and serves as the cutoff man. He has the ability to "cut off" the ball and try to throw out a different base runner. The outfielder throwing the ball home aims at the cutoff man. And that's where we get the phrase "hitting the cutoff man." In a game in July 2004, "hitting the cutoff man" was taken to the extreme. The San Diego Padres were hosting the Kansas City Royals when a fly ball was hit to right field. There was a runner on third who tagged up to score. The Kansas City right fielder, Desi Relaford, fired a bullet right at the cutoff man, second baseman Ken Harvey. Only, Harvey was on his knees facing home plate. He was ducking so that the throw could go past him directly home. As luck would have it, *plunk!* The ball hit him squarely in the back. Nobody had hit the cutoff man more perfectly. And nobody got hurt, either.

Is it a double triple or a triple double?

In April 2006 at Washington State University, the home team was hosting the Gonzaga University Zags in baseball. In the second inning, the Cougars of Washington State had runners on first and second with nobody out. The batter Zach Franklin lined the ball hard and it was caught by the Zags' first baseman Bobby Carlson. The batter was out. Both runners were off at the crack of the bat. Carlson simply stepped on first, and threw to second to complete a triple play. But the weird part is what happened in the very next inning. Again, the Cougars had runners on first and second with nobody out. This time the batter was Jay Miller. Would you believe he also lined it to first, and again Carlson stepped on first and threw to second? This time the throw was high and to the third base side. Gonzaga shortstop Aaron McGuinness leaped into the air, caught the ball, and in one smooth motion tagged out the runner trying to slide back into second base. Another triple play! Triple plays in back-to-back innings! Only once in major league history did a team turn two triple plays in the same game. The Minnesota Twins did it to the Boston Red Sox in 1990, but not in consecutive innings. And we'll let math fans decide what you call it when a team called the Twins turns two triple plays.

EXTRA INNINGS

If a batted ball goes off home plate and then into fair territory, is it fair or foul? The answer is: every part of every base is in fair territory, so it's a fair ball.

Talk about a "twin killing." In a playoff game at Shea Stadium in October 2006, Mets catcher Paul Lo Duca tagged out Jeff Kent of the Dodgers as he tried to score. Then he immediately tagged out J.D. Drew trying to score right behind Kent. Two outs at the plate on the same play just seconds apart. It was a "bang bang double play."

Who hit the longest home run ever? Nobody knows for sure, but some have suggested that it was Mickey Mantle who hit a ball more than 600 feet in Detroit in 1960.

No time to go get a hot dog. In September 1919, the Giants beat the Phillies 6–1. The game took fifty-one minutes to play! It was the fastest major league game in history.

It was a lot harder to draw a base on balls when baseball was first invented in the 1800s. Instead of four balls, a batter had to get nine.

Can you catch a baseball thrown out of an airplane? The manager of the Brooklyn Dodgers, Wilbert Robinson, wanted to find out. So in 1915 during an exhibition game in Daytona Beach, Florida, he tried to make the catch. But somebody substituted a grapefruit for the ball, and it splattered all over him!

BASKETBALL

March Madness is what they call the NCAA Basketball Tournament. It got that name because of the buzzer-beating upsets that can occur at any time throughout the tournament. But why limit the madness to college basketball or to March? Lots of crazy stuff happens in all the other months. And as you're about to find out, it's not limited to the game itself. It can start before the opening tip-off with the National Anthem. I've seen some weird clothing malfunctions, and baskets of every shape and size. How about scoring the game-tying hoop in a championship game while lying on your back? And during halftime, I've seen hairy backs and wedding proposals that didn't end too well. The fans are pretty wacky as well. Would you believe one guy wanted to stay in prison longer because of basketball? It's all true. So grab a seat, start reading, and have a ball. Just make sure you don't double dribble!

A REAL Larry Bird fan

In October 2005, a convict in Oklahoma was given a thirty-year prison sentence. His name was Eric James Torpy. And he wasn't happy. Would you be? Well, it turns out he didn't want a thirty-year sentence, he wanted thirty-three years! His favorite basketball player was Larry Bird, the great Boston Celtic. Bird wore number 33, so he wanted a thirty-three-year sentence in "honor" of his hero. Authorities claimed it was the first time someone ever asked for more jail time. The judge was happy to increase his sentence by three years, and Torpy was happy to accept it. Is that a "win-win" or a "lose-lose" proposition?

Who needs to see?

In an NBA basketball game in January 2005, The Toronto Raptors were hosting the Phoenix Suns. Mo Peterson, a headband-wearing Raptor, was near the foul line, preparing to make his move

toward the basket. Then, two things happened. He was fouled and his headband slipped over his eyes, so he couldn't see. No trouble for Mo. He continued to drive toward the hoop and made the layup while completely blindfolded.

Keep your eye on which ball?

In a college basketball game in St. Louis, between the St. Louis Billikens and the Arizona Wildcats in December 2003, Salim Stoudamire, for Arizona, was standing at the foul line for some crucial foul shots late in the game. In sports they always tell you to "keep your eye on the ball." Well, as Stoudamire prepared to shoot his free throw, a rubber ball was thrown from the stands. It bounced onto the court and hit Stoudamire in the hip as he was shooting. He continued his motion and made the foul shot. Talk about concentration. Would you believe Arizona won the game by that one point?

Quick-change artist

In February 2005, the Denver Nuggets were hosting the Utah Jazz. Early in the game, Nuggets rookie Carmelo Anthony realized his shorts were on backwards. So he simply dropped his shorts to the floor, turned them around, and pulled them back up. His long jersey prevented anything embarrassing, but it didn't stop all his teammates on the bench from laughing.

Team loyalty

Remember the baseball fan who won the "Hairiest Back" competition? Well, it's not just baseball fans who are proud of their back hair. During halftime at Chicago Bulls games, there is often a group of overweight men called the Matadors (Get it? Bulls . . . Matadors?) dancing on the court. These guys aren't particularly graceful, and it's funny watching them do their thing.

During a game in February 2005, one of the Matadors wasn't wearing his shirt, and he was quite hairy. When the camera zoomed in, he had the Chicago Bulls logo shaved onto his hairy back. Now that's team spirit!

I don't!

During halftime of a basketball game in Washington in February 2004, fans were treated to an interesting contest. A random fan was chosen from the crowd and was blindfolded. She wandered around the court trying to find the mascot, who was holding a prize. The crowd cheered or booed depending on how close she was to finding the mascot.

They often staged this contest during the Washington Wizards games, so fans thought it was business as usual. But this night, when the fan found the mascot, the mascot took off his costume, got on one knee, and proposed marriage. The "not-so-blushing bride-to-be" stood there for a moment and then ran off the court. The scoreboard flashed the message: "She Said No!" The crowd was stunned. Turns out, it was all one big joke that was played on the crowd by the people who run the contests in Washington.

I guess they were watching in Orlando. The following year, the night before Valentine's Day in 2005, at halftime of an Orlando Magic game, a man dropped to one knee on the court and said, "Joy, will you marry me?" Joy ran off the court. Another turn-down. And another hoax. It was all a joke set up by the Orlando Magic marketing people. The next night in New Orleans, there was another on-court proposal. The woman jumped on top of the man and starting kissing him as they rolled around on the floor. I'm guessing, this time, she said yes.

Eventful evening

In December 2004, Jerry Stackhouse of the Dallas Mavericks sang the National Anthem in front of a packed stadium before the Mavericks game with the Boston Celtics. He sang the song perfectly. Unfortunately, the rest of the night didn't go so well. He got ejected by the referees with a couple of minutes left in the game after getting hit with his second technical foul. This night, for Jerry, had a much better start than ending.

Oh, say, can't you sing?

At the New Orleans Hornets game in February 2004, the National Anthem was sung by Terry Barrileaux. Actually, she was supposed to sing it, but she forgot the words. She just stopped and asked, "What?" Then she said, "Y'all just have to sing along with me." With that, the public address announcer at courtside, Jim Rumsfeld, got on his microphone and started singing. All the fans started to sing along as well. At that point, one of the NBA referees walked over to Terry and pointed to one of the scoreboards in the arena where the words of the anthem were displayed. Now the anthem singer could sing along with everyone else!

Wet your whistle

Something you don't see every day: In January 2004 at an NBA game in Dallas, referee Joey Crawford displayed his generous side. During a time-out, he took cash out of his pocket and handed it to a beer vendor. He pointed to a couple of fans and told the vendor to give them beers. Normally a ref dishes out fouls, but free beer?

38

Basketball

Lying down on the job

In March 2005, Blake Hoffarber made one of the most incredible shots in the history of high school basketball. It came during the Minnesota high school championship game in Minneapolis. Eastview was playing against Hopkins and leading by three. Hoffarber made a 3-point shot that tied the game for Hopkins and forced overtime. That's when the craziness began. Eastview was leading by two in overtime and just moments away from the championship. Hopkins tried a long pass, and while scrambling for the ball, Hoffarber fell down. Amazingly the ball bounced right to him and he caught it while he was lying on the floor. He was eighteen feet away from the basket so he just flung the ball into the air while lying down, and the ball went swish! It tied the game at 58–58 and forced a second overtime. Eastview must have been so stunned that they were barely able to score in the overtime. Just two points. Hoffarber and Hopkins went on to win the state championship in overtime 71–60. How hard was Hoffarber's shot to make? He went to the gym to try to do it again. Same thing, lying on the floor. It took him twenty-one tries to make it.

Our hero

For seventeen-year-old Jason McElwain, it was a script right out of Hollywood. In February 2006, he was the team manager for Greece Athena High School in a Rochester, New York, suburb. During his team's final home game, he finally got into his first and only game of the season. Jason is autistic and didn't even speak until he was five years old. When he got off the bench to enter the game, it was a heartwarming moment for his family and friends. But that's just the beginning of the story. In the final minutes of the game, he couldn't miss a basket. He hit one 3-point shot after another, to the delight of the crowd. In a four-minute span, he scored 20 points! The crowd went wild. At the end of the game they stormed the court and placed Jason on their shoulders. And there's more. All sorts of movie companies started calling. They wanted to turn Jason's story into a real Hollywood script. The following month,

Basketball

President Bush was heading to upstate New York to make a speech. He had Air Force One touch down at an airport near Jason's home. He too wanted to meet this incredible teenager. Jason said it was a dream come true!

OVERTIME

The slam dunk is so common in basketball that we take it for granted. Would you believe it took over 50 years for somebody to dunk a basketball? That's right. The game of basketball was first played in the 1890s, and it wasn't until 1946 that a player at Oklahoma University, Bob Kurland, dunked a ball in a game. Of course, he was seven feet tall! It took another thirty-eight years for a woman to dunk in a college game. It happened in 1984, when Georgeann Wells-Blackwell did it for West Virginia. She was six feet seven inches tall.

Talk about highs and lows. The Pistons were involved in both. In December 1983, the Detroit Pistons beat the Denver Nuggets 186–184 in three overtimes. It was the highest-scoring game in NBA history. If Detroit hadn't missed a ton of foul shots, they would have scored more than 200 points. Thirty-three years earlier, the Detroit Pistons played in Fort Wayne, Indiana. The Fort Wayne Pistons beat the Minneapolis Lakers in

November 1950. It was the lowest-scoring game in NBA history. Fort Wayne won it 19–18!

Who was the tallest basketball player of all time? That honor belongs to Suleiman Ali Nashnush. He played for the country of Libya in 1962. He was eight feet and half an inch tall. I'm guessing he could dunk the ball without jumping!

You can get a technical foul in a basketball game for doing all sorts of things, such as kicking the ball or cursing at the official. But this may be a first. In February 1998, in Rochester, New York, Point Park University basketball coach Bob Rager ate a big meal before the game. It was Italian food loaded with garlic. Garlic can make your breath smell really bad. During the game he got into an argument with the referee. At one point during the heated discussion, Rager just exhaled into the face of the ref. The referee called a technical foul on Rager . . . for breathing!

FOOTBALL

Okay, so football is pretty easy. You have to move the ball across the goal line to score six points, or you can settle for kicking a field goal for three. Nothing too complicated. Except when you figure that there are twenty-two players on the field, a zillion confusing rules, and one football that isn't perfectly round. Let the fun begin.

"Back" is a big word in football. You've got your quarterback, halfback, fullback, and defensive back. But wait until you read about how players' backs figure into some weird plays.

Speaking of weird, how about the official calling a penalty on the marching band? They're not even on the field! And most people think that crossing the goal line is a big deal in football. But you'd better be careful that you actually cross the line. You'll soon see why.

And how about a doubleheader in football, ever hear of that? You're about to. So, "first and ten, do it again." It's time to kick off the football chapter. Don't forget to put your helmet on.

It's not over till it's over

In football, a play isn't over until the referee blows his whistle. It was something to think about in November 2003, when Mississippi's Rebels were playing a college football game against South Carolina. It was South Carolina's ball when, late in the third quarter, they handed off the ball to Daccus Turman on the 29-yard line. He started running when he was grabbed by Mississippi linebacker Ken Bournes. Bournes appeared to tackle him in a bear hug as they fell to the ground. Bournes jumped up to celebrate, pointing both hands toward the sky. Except, it wasn't a tackle. When Bournes fell to the ground, *his* back was touching the field. He brought Turman down on top of him. Turman's back or knee never hit the ground. So while Bournes was jumping around in celebration, Turman simply got up and ran 29 yards for the touchdown!

Here's another one involving a "back." In September 2005, in Tuscaloosa, Alabama, Alabama was hosting Southern Mississippi in a college football game. Southern Miss was dominating the action, leading 21–10 with just a few seconds left before the half. Alabama was faced with a fourth down, so quarterback Brodie Croyle lofted a deep pass toward the end zone. Alabama wide receiver Tyrone Prothro leaped into the air at the same time as Southern Mississippi defensive back Jasper Faulk. The ball was over both their heads and started to come down behind Faulk. Prothro reached around Faulk and caught the ball by pinning it to Faulk's back as the two of them fell to the turf. It was ruled a completion, an amazing catch. At first they called it a touchdown, but then they marked the ball at the 1-yard line. Alabama scored seconds later, and Southern Mississippi never scored another point. Alabama went on to win the game 30–21. The "behind the back" catch was clearly the turning point of the game!

This one was even crazier. In December 2005, the Alamo Bowl was played in San Antonio between Nebraska and Michigan. Nebraska was leading 32–28 when Michigan tried one final play. They were on their side of the field, around the 35-yard line, when quarterback Chad Henne threw a short pass to Jason Avant. As time ran out, the Michigan players kept lateraling the ball to one another to keep the play alive. In truth, they were going the wrong way, and kept losing yards, but the game wasn't over yet. At one point it looked like one of the Michigan players was down with the ball, which would have ended the play and the game. But it turns out his knee never touched the ground. So Tyler Eckers of Michigan started running with the ball. By this time, both teams thought the game was over and all of the players and coaches started coming onto the field. It was a mess. And Eckers just kept on running. The officials didn't say a thing. They didn't blow their whistles, and they didn't throw any penalty flags. And all the while Eckers kept getting closer to the goal line, and the winning touchdown. Finally, Titus Brothers of Nebraska pushed him out of bounds just thirteen yards shy of the end zone, saving the day for Nebraska; it would have been one of the craziest touchdowns ever scored!

Taking a knee

In football, if you put your knee down, the play is over. Oftentimes it's done intentionally. For example, one team kicks off to the other and the ball is caught in the end zone. Rather than trying to run the ball out of his end zone, a player may decide to kneel down. It's ruled a touchback, which means the offense then starts at the 20-yard line. Well, in October 2004, Georgia was hosting

Louisiana State University in college football. In the third quarter, Georgia kicked off and LSU's Xavier Carter caught the football about five yards deep into the end zone. He started to run the ball out and then thought better of it. So he kneeled down on the ground. One slight problem. He had

crossed the goal line, and he kneeled at the 1-yard line. Oops! That's where the LSU offense had to begin, rather than at the 20 if he had correctly kneeled in the end zone.

There was another goal line "mishap" that was even wilder. It occurred in a high school all-star game in January 2005 in San Antonio. DeSean Jackson, from the Long Beach California Poly Mustangs, caught a pass at the 40-yard line and had clear sailing to the end zone. But just before he got to the goal line, he decided to leap into the air and put on a show as he scored his touchdown. Unfortunately for DeSean, he miscalculated his jump and he leaped too soon. Instead of landing in the end zone, he came down at the 1-yard line. Not only wasn't it a touchdown, he was assessed a 15-yard penalty for showboating!

Let's play two

Did you hear the one about the college football team that won two games on the same day?

In October 2005, the Northwestern College Eagles in St. Paul, Minnesota, did something that had never been done before. They played a doubleheader. Not in baseball, in football. And not against the same team. Two different teams. They spent their afternoon shutting out the Trinity Bible College Lions 59–0. Then they played a night game and beat the Macalester Scots 47–14. Not a bad day for Northwestern: they outscored their opponents 106 to 14 in one day. The only difficulty? They had to play the second game in dirty pants. Their small college couldn't afford two sets of football pants, so they played in the same clothes.

Getting his kicks

At a Canadian Football League game in October 2005, one lucky fan got to try kicking field goals for fame and fortune. Twenty-five-year-old Brian Diesbourg lined up at the 20-yard line. If he made the kick, he'd win a thousand dollars. His kick was long enough, but it just missed to the right. So he moved back to the 30-yard line and tried to kick for a digital camera. Same thing. Wide right. So he moved back to the 40. Now the prize was a high-definition TV. Again the kick was long enough, but again it was a little wide to the right.

Football

So they gave him one last chance from the 50-yard line. This time the kick was right down the middle and it was good! His prize? A cool one million dollars. The amazing part? Up until that day, he had never kicked a football in his life.

OVERTIME

In September 2004, Bethune-Cookman College was playing Grambling State University in Cincinnati. The Grambling band was located up in the stands, and was playing during the action. A band isn't supposed to do that. So the referee called a 15-yard "unsportsmanlike" penalty on the band!

Quick, does an NFL football weigh more or less than one pound? Time's up. The correct answer is less. It weighs between fourteen and fifteen ounces. A pound is sixteen ounces.

The longest field goal ever kicked in a game was booted by Ove Johansson. It happened in October 1976 in Abilene, Texas. Kicking for the Abilene Christian Wildcats, he kicked it an amazing sixty-nine yards. That's six yards longer than the NFL record.

Football

So you're wondering why a football is just about the only ball that isn't round. Well, football is derived from the sport of rugby, which also uses an oblong ball. So why does a rugby ball have such an odd shape? It was made by wrapping a pig's bladder in leather. And that's the shape it turned out to be.

In September 1990, Howard Griffith, a senior fullback for the University of Illinois, had quite a day. The Fighting Illini hosted the Salukis of Southern Illinois that day, and Illinois won the game 56–21. Griffith scored an amazing eight touchdowns! Too bad he couldn't kick extra points too, because Griffith scored every point for his team, except for the 8 extra points. And yes, his 48 points is a record for points scored by one player in a college football game.

SOCCER

Here's an easy question: what's the most popular sport in the world? It's football, but not American football. Soccer. There's an easy explanation. Soccer is played in more countries than any other sport. And this sport seems to have the craziest, most passionate fans. That may explain the wacky stories. . . . But when you hear about the Newcastle "team," you'll think some of the players are pretty nutty as well. In the following pages you'll find tough goalies, firecrackers, chickens, garbage cans, and pizza, all in the name of soccer! So, lace up your cleats and remember the number one rule in soccer: you're not allowed to use your hands, except of course to turn the pages.

Gooooooal!

In July 2004, Greece was playing Portugal in the European Soccer Championship game. One "genius" ran onto the field during the action and the officials started to chase him off the field. This "brilliant" fan tried to get away from the authorities by running directly into the soccer goal. He was stopped, of course, by the net. In essence he "scored" himself directly to jail!

Who you calling chicken?

Remember the rooster who caused a ruckus at a baseball game? Well, here's what happens when a disgruntled fan starts to get cocky. In October 2003, in Rio de Janeiro, Brazil, to show his unhappiness with his local soccer club, a dissatisfied fan brought a bunch of live chickens to the team's practice session and tossed them onto the field. He was trying to make the statement that his favorite soccer team lacked toughness and played like "chickens." Turns out the fan lacked some toughness of his own. The players weren't happy with his actions and started to run after him. The fan was pretty "chicken" himself, and ran as fast as he could, but the players caught up to him and showed their displeasure by trying to beat him up. Calm was eventually restored, but not before the "feathers flew."

Toughest goaltender in the world?

During a soccer game in Treviso, Italy, in February 2004, Treviso was hosting Verona, with Treviso leading 1–0 in the first half. Verona was on the attack, trying to score the tying goal, when an idiotic fan threw a huge firecracker onto the soccer

field right next to Treviso goaltender Jean-François Gillet. The explosion knocked out Gillet, and, at that very moment while he was lying on the field, Verona kicked the ball into the net. They disallowed the goal. Gillet got up and he finished the game! Not only that, but the goalie registered a shutout. Treviso won the game 2–nothing, and Gillet showed that he is one tough goalie.

Bull's-eye

One of the most perfect soccer kicks I ever saw occurred in a game in New Jersey in 2005. Colombia was playing Panama. One of the players kicked a marvelous shot that missed the goal completely. It soared way past the net and landed right in a trash can on the fly. His accuracy wasn't so hot. I guess you could call the shot "garbage."

Heated battle

It's not unusual to see a couple of players go at it on the soccer field. Occasionally punches get thrown. What is unusual is what happened in Newcastle, England, in April 2005. Newcastle hadn't lost a game all season, and was playing against Aston Villa. Newcastle was on the verge of losing, when tempers flared. Lee Bowyer started punching Kieron Dyer. But they were on the same team! There they were, two teammates wearing the same striped shirts, flailing away at each other. An opposing player from Aston Villa had to come over and break them up. It's not unusual for a referee to "red card" two players for an incident on the field. A red card means the player is thrown out of the game. Normally if two red cards are issued at once, it's one player from each team who gets ejected. The ref proceeded to toss out the two squabbling teammates. So Newcastle had to play the rest of the game with two players less than Aston Villa. Does it come as any surprise that Newcastle lost its first game of the year that day 3–nothing?

OVERTIME

In March 2005, Norwegian soccer player Bard Erik Olsen was all set to retire. But the team bribed him to continue his career. They told him if he continued to play, he could have as much pizza as he wanted to eat. Bard loved his pizza, and couldn't pass up such a yummy deal. Turns out, it was not the oddest agreement in the history of Norwegian soccer. One time a player was traded to another team for his weight in shrimp! (They must love food and sports in Norway!)

In September 2006, the Yale Bulldogs were playing the North Carolina Tar Heels in a women's soccer game. On the game's opening kick, Yael Averbuch of the Tar Heels kicked the ball more than 50 yards and it went into the net. She had scored a goal just four seconds into the game! It was the fastest goal in the history of college soccer. And Averbuch also scored the game-winning goal! North Carolina won the game 4–0. In fact it might

have been the fastest goal ever scored. Hakan Sükür of Turkey, in 2002, scored eleven seconds into a World Cup game against South Korea. That's seven whole seconds slower than Yael Averbuch!

In a World Cup qualifying match in Australia, in April 2001, Archie Thompson of Australia set a world record by scoring thirteen goals in one game. Australia beat American Samoa 31–0. At first the final score was reported as 32–0. There were so many goals that the scorekeeper lost count.

GOLF

When it comes to individual sports, there is no sport more individual than golf. You're not trying to hit the ball while somebody is throwing it ninety miles an hour, like in baseball. Nobody is trying to guard you, as in basketball. And thank goodness they don't have tackle golf. You are all alone, just you and your little golf ball trying to tame a golf course. And some of the craziest stuff happens all the time. How about a pro scoring a 23 on one hole. Or a player throwing a club up in the air. It came down and hit him in the head. As you'll soon see, guys have tried to golf across waterfalls and even across entire countries. Then there's the noise factor. It's supposed to be completely quiet when somebody is swinging his golf club, but it doesn't always work out that way. So grab a club and swing away. But if you hit a bad shot that might hit somebody, don't forget to yell, "Fore!" We don't want anyone to get hurt.

Much longer than a par 5

Almost every golf hole is either a par 3, 4, or 5. Par is the normal score a golfer should get on a hole. It always includes two putts. So for a par 3, you're expected to hit the ball onto the green with your tee shot, and then take two putts to get the ball into the hole. If you score one lower than par, that's a birdie. And that's really good. One over a par? That's a bogey. Not so hot. But what's par for a golf hole that stretches across an entire country? In the summer of 2004, Andre Tolme golfed across Mongolia. All 1,200 miles. He figured out the par was around 11,880! It took him three months to finish the golf hole. And he only lost 509 golf balls along the way.

How about trying to drive a golf ball from one country to another? That's what pro golfer John Daly tried to do in August 2005. He stood in Canada and tried to drive a golf ball 342 yards to America. In between lay the famed Horseshoe Falls of Niagara Falls. Daly has driven a golf ball farther than 342 yards on the PGA Tour, but on this day he "gripped it and ripped it," which is his style of play. He powered twenty drives toward the

U.S. and all twenty drives wound up wet. It will probably go down as the biggest water hazard in the history of golf!

Good news, bad news

Can good and bad happen on the same shot? Count the ways.

At the 1934 U.S. Open in Pennsylvania, Bobby Cruickshank hit his ball into the water on the eleventh hole. (That's bad.) But the ball hit a rock and bounced onto dry land. (That's good.) He was so happy he threw his club into the air. (That's bad.) It came down and conked him on the head, knocking him to the ground. (That's even worse.) He survived to finish the round. (That's good.) He didn't win. (That's bad.) But he did have a great story to tell, and nobody got hurt! (That's outstanding!)

If at first you don't succeed

At the 1938 U.S. Open in New Jersey, a golfer from California named Ray Ainsley had quite an adventure. On the par 4 sixteenth hole, he hit his

ball into a stream. So he climbed into the water and tried to hit the ball. Again. And again. It was a swift-moving stream and this took a great deal of effort, not to mention time. For half an hour, poor

Ray Ainsley searched for his ball at the bottom of the stream and flailed away, trying to hit it out of there. When all was said and done, he scored a U.S. Open record 19 on the hole. That is fifteen shots over par! Ainsley didn't have to go to all that trouble. He could have removed the ball from the stream and taken a one-stroke penalty. But amazingly, he said he didn't know that. He thought he had to play the ball "as it lies." If he had done that, he would have saved a whole bunch of strokes. But then again, he wouldn't have wound up in the record books.

There is a tiny bit of good news for Ainsley. While his 19 is a record for a U.S. Open, it's not the all-time high for a pro golf tournament. That honor belongs to Tommy Armour. At the 1927 Shawnee Open in Pennsylvania, he shot an all-time high of 23 on one hole! And it's not as if he had been playing poorly. Just the week before, he won the U.S. Open.

Record setter

In June 2005, before a baseball game in Kansas City, pro golfer David Ogrin tried to set a record.

He stood at home plate hitting golf balls as fast as he could. His friend would place a ball in front of him and he'd swing. It was very impressive how fast they were going. In sixty seconds Ogrin managed to hit seventy-seven golf balls. Nobody had ever hit seventy-seven golf balls in a minute before. Ogrin had himself a record but unfortunately not much else. His earnings for the 2005 pro golf season: a big fat zero dollars!

Silence, please

Golf is just about the only sport where you need total silence when the athlete is doing his thing. It doesn't always work out that way. I once saw Tiger Woods back away from a putt because there were loud birds in a tree creating a huge racket. Then there was Loren Roberts, who was teeing off at the Western Open in Illinois in July 2004. Right in the middle of his backswing, a teenager set off a loud air horn. Roberts had to stop. The teenager was last seen running away with other golf fans in pursuit!

Do as you're told!

In January 2005, Tiger Woods was filming a TV commercial for Nike. They asked him to hit a golf ball toward a camera that was situated about

fifty yards away. Maybe it wasn't smart asking the world's number-one golfer to hit a golf ball at an expensive piece of equipment. Tiger hit a perfect shot (bull's-eye) right into the camera lens, breaking it. Tiger chuckled and proclaimed, "You said to try to hit the camera."

Nailing a birdie

At the U.S. Open in Pinehurst, North Carolina, in June 2005, golfer David Toms hit a fascinating approach shot to the eighteenth green. There was a small bird sitting on the green, and Toms's shot from the fairway landed softly and rolled right up to the bird, gently hitting it. The bird immediately flew away. Toms proceeded to roll in his putt for a birdie. So in effect, he got two birdies on the same hole!

You go, girl!

Fifty-nine is a magic number in pro golf. It's the lowest score ever recorded on the pro golf tour. Only three men in the history of golf have ever shot that score in a PGA event. Even more amazing, only one woman has ever done it. Annika Sorenstam shot a 59 at the Moon Valley Country Club in Phoenix in March 2001. On one hole her birdie putt lipped out of the cup, or else she would have shot a 58!

SUDDEN DEATH

Why do they yell "fore" when somebody hits a bad shot? According to the U.S. Golf Association, it's a shortened version of "before" or "afore." It's an old Scottish warning meaning "look out ahead."

In golf, if you hit a mammoth 300-yard drive, or make a two-foot putt, it counts for the same. One shot. And sometimes that one little shot can be so agonizing. At the U.S. Open in June 2001, Stewart Cink had a little eighteen-inch putt on the last hole. He didn't think it meant much at the time, but he was wrong. He didn't take it seriously, and he missed. It turns out he finished one shot off the lead, and missed his chance to get into a play-off. Those eighteen little inches may have cost him $575,000 dollars, the difference between first place and third, which is where he wound up.

Golf is a nice leisurely sport. Players take four to five hours to play eighteen holes. In December

1981, the American track star Steve Scott wanted to play a little faster. So he took two golf clubs and played eighteen holes in just twenty-nine minutes. And he shot a respectable 92!

Hawaiian golfer Michelle Wie qualified to play in an official amateur event at the age of ten. Why not? She shot an amazing 64 that year!

TENNIS

Tennis is known as a refined and tasteful sport. For example, at Wimbledon they don't refer to the players as guys or gals. It's the "gentlemen's final" or the "ladies' championship." Of course, what happens on the court can be anything but classy. Players yell and scream at umpires. I've seen players push each other in the middle of a match. And, of course, weird stuff happens just like in all the other sports. For example, can you be penalized for having beads in your hair? Well, it all depends on what happens to the beads. And you would think keeping score would be easy. Not always the case. So grab a racket and enjoy a few sets of tennis. Just remember to keep your eye on the ball, not to mention the scoreboard.

Hats off

I thought tennis player Max Mirnyi of Belarus made a terrific move at the U.S. Open in 2005. It came during the doubles championship. He was teamed with Jonas Björkman, and they were taking on the American Bryan twins, Bob and Mike. During the middle of one point, Mirnyi's hat fell off his head. All in one motion, he reached behind his back with his left hand and caught his hat, putting it back on his head. At the same time, he was hitting a ball with the racket in his right hand. A terrific maneuver. If only the rest of the day had gone as well. Mirnyi and Björkman lost that point as well as the match. But at least Max saved his hat!

Flipping your lid

At the 2006 U.S. Open in Queens, New York, Russian Maria Sharapova beat Justine Henin-Hardenne of Belgium in the final 6–4, 6–4. It was Sharapova's first U.S. Open victory. When they handed her the trophy, she jumped up and down and held the trophy aloft. She didn't realize the metal trophy had a lid, and it came crashing down on her head before hitting the ground. She could have knocked herself out with her own victory dance! Thankfully, nobody got hurt!

Simple math

At the 2003 U.S. Open, Tamarine Tanasugarn of Thailand was playing a third-round match against Daniela Hantuchova of Slovakia. Late in the second set, Hantuchova hit the ball long and Tanasugarn let out a loud shriek, jumped into the air, turned around, and started walking toward the net for the traditional end-of-match handshake. One minor problem: the score was now five games to three, and you need six games to win the set. She was off by a full game. Later, with the score five games to four, Hantuchova hit the ball into the net, and now it was time for Tanasugarn to celebrate. She was much more subdued this time. No yelling. Just a little mock dance to make fun of her own lack of math skills.

Simpler math

At Wimbledon in 2004, American Venus Williams was playing Karolina Sprem of Croatia in a second-round match. During the second-set tiebreaker, Sprem served and the ball went wide. It was called out by a line judge. But the two continued to play, and Sprem "won the point." She went on to win the match, and nobody complained about the mistake. She had clearly won a point that she hadn't earned. In other sports a coach might have argued, but tennis is the only sport that doesn't allow coaching during a match!

Battle of the sexes

So who would win a tennis match between a top-ranked male player and a female champion? Before you say the man, let me tell you about Bobby Riggs. He had been the number-one player in the world in the '30s and '40s. But in 1973 he was 55 years old. He challenged the top-ranked women's player in the world, thirty-year-old Margaret Court. The match was played on Mother's Day in 1973 in Ramona, California. Riggs easily won the match, 6–2, 6–1. At the time, Billie Jean King was one of the greatest tennis players in history. She had won Wimbledon earlier that year. Now it was her turn. King was twenty-nine when they squared off in Houston in September 1973. Who won this time? King won in a cakewalk, 6–4, 6–3, 6–3. The match was played at the

Astrodome, and an estimated 50 million watched on television. In person, the match drew the biggest tennis crowd of all time: more than 34,000.

Bad hair day

Tennis player Venus Williams often wears beads in her hair when she plays. During the Australian Open, in the middle of a match, a strand of beads broke and scattered around the court. She was penalized a point for her wayward beads!

TIEBREAKER

Andy Roddick has the fastest serve on record at 155 miles per hour in a 2004 Davis Cup match in Charleston, South Carolina. Venus Williams owns the women's record: 127.4 in Zurich, Switzerland, in 1998.

Why is a tennis score of zero called love? It comes from the French word for egg: *l'oeuf.* An egg is shaped like a zero, and when you say *l'oeuf,* it sounds like "love." Sounds better than "the score is now 40–egg."

The youngest Wimbledon champ? Charlotte "Lottie" Dod of Great Britain, just fifteen years old in 1887. The youngest to ever win a match at the U.S. Open? Mary Joe Fernandez. She was only fourteen when she beat Sara Gomer in 1985.

At Wimbledon in 1995, Jeff Tarango was so upset with the chair umpire that he stormed off the court, thus losing his match to Alexander Mronz. Tarango's wife was even more upset. She went over and slapped the chair umpire in the face! Ouch.

American Vince Spadea owns a dubious distinction. At the beginning of 2000, he lost the first seventeen matches he played. On clay, on grass, on hard courts. No matter what surface he played on, he lost. His losing streak, including 1999, was twenty-one matches, the longest in pro tennis history. He finally won a match at Wimbledon in June 2000, breaking an eight-month losing streak!

Olympics

So, here's the deal with the Olympics. It only comes around every four years. Oh sure, since they alternate between the summer and winter games, there's one every two years. But if you're an athlete in, let's say, gymnastics, and if you don't do so hot, you've got to wait four years to try to do better. There's nothing else like it. In baseball, the phrase is famous: "Wait 'til next year." There's always next season to look forward to. There was a terrific football player named Duane Thomas who played for the Dallas Cowboys. When his team made it to the Super Bowl he said, "What's the big deal? They've got another Super Bowl next year, don't they?"

That's the point. In the Olympics, "next year" is four looooooong years away. So if you wake up the morning of your gymnastics event and you've got a cold, or your leg hurts, that's the breaks. See you in four years, and hopefully your leg feels better by then.

I've heard about some crazy stuff in the Olympics. Did you know they once had an Olympic event in tug-of-war? Pigeons haven't fared too well in the Olympics. Wait until you read why. There was a rower who was so excited that he won a gold medal that he threw his medal into the lake by mistake. And cheating? All kinds of stuff! One fencer was really creative until he got caught!

As for the Olympians, you'll read about the "perfect 10" at one end of the spectrum, and "Eddie the Eagle," who was anything but perfect, yet everybody loved him. Or nearly everyone.

So, don't wait four years to read this. Get going, and hopefully when it comes to reading about the Olympics, you'll feel as if you've won the gold medal. But hang on to it tightly.

Upon further review!

Stella Walsh was born in Poland in 1911. Her real name was Stanislawa Walasiewiczowna, but that wasn't the only "change" in her life. She lived in the U.S. and, in 1932, she competed for her native Poland at the Olympics in Los Angeles and won the 100-meter dash. She died in 1980. After her death, when they examined her, it turned out she was really a man!

Oops!

At the 2006 Olympic Winter Games in Torino, Italy, they held a new event called the snowboard cross. Four competitors ski downhill side by side, making multiple jumps and turns. In the final race, the first to cross the finish line wins the gold medal. Twenty-year-old snowboarder Lindsey Jacobellis, from Stratton, Vermont, was cruising to the gold. She had a fifty-yard lead. The gold medal was hers. But on her next to last jump she tried to get fancy. She did an extra jump and crashed to the snow. As she was scrambling to get up and finish the race, Tanja Frieden of Switzerland zipped past her to win the gold. Lindsey had to settle for the silver. Said Lindsey, "I messed up. It happens."

Another oops!

At the 1956 Summer Games in Melbourne, Australia, eighteen-year-old Soviet rower Vyacheslav Ivanov won the single sculls. That's basically one person in a rowboat. He was so excited that he tossed his gold medal into the air. It fell into the lake and "drowned." Nobody ever saw it again.

It's not whether you win or lose

It's not really known who first said, "It's not whether you win or lose, but how you play the game." But it was never more appropriate than at the 2006 Olympic Winter Games in Torino, Italy. Ivan Borisov was the entire Olympic team from Kyrgyzstan. He's an alpine skier, and because he was the only representative of his country, he got to carry the flag at the opening ceremony. When he skied in the giant slalom, he missed a gate. Normally when a skier does that, he just stops. He's finished. He's disqualified. But Borisov wasn't going to let a missed gate spoil his Olympic experience. So he trudged back up the hill to the gate he missed. While he was doing that, another skier came speeding by and nearly hit him. Borisov then completed his run a full forty-three seconds behind the leader. In a sport decided by fractions of a second, forty-three seconds is a lifetime behind. It didn't matter to Ivan. He wanted to finish what he had started. When he got to the bottom of the hill, he pumped his fists as if he had won the event!

"Athlons"

The Olympics are famous for "athlons." In the winter games, they have the biathlon (two sports in one). In the summer games, they have the triathlon (three sports), pentathlon (five sports), and the granddaddy of them all, the decathlon (ten sports in one!). How many do you know? Well, the biathlon combines cross-country skiing and rifle shooting. The triathlon is swimming, running, and bicycling. The pentathlon is horseback riding (show jumping), fencing, rifle shooting, swimming, and running. And in the decathlon, which is competed over two days, you have the 100-meter run, long jump, shot put, high jump, 400-meter run, 110-meter hurdles, discus throw, pole vault, javelin throw, and (finally) the 1500-meter run. Whew.

So, in a biathlon a competitor skis and he shoots a rifle, but not at the same time. First he skis a loop on the course, then he comes to a shooting range and aims at five targets, and then he goes to ski some more. He alternates skiing and shooting until the race is over. During the 2006 Olympic Winter Games in Torino, Italy, Jay Hakkinen from Alaska was the best American biathlete. He came in tenth in one race, which was the best American finish ever in a biathlon at the Olympics. During his second race, he went to shoot at his five targets and missed them all. That is highly unusual. In that race, when you miss a target you have to ski a 150-meter penalty loop. So Jay had to ski five extra loops, which would put him way behind in the race. He was so mad at himself for missing those targets, he lost count and skied six loops by mistake, putting him even farther behind. No wonder he finished in 80th place. But he wasn't the only one who had problems. In another race, while they were all lined up at the shooting range, Gunn Margit Andreassen of Norway was hitting the targets. There was one minor problem. She was shooting at somebody else's targets by mistake! She missed all five of her own. The targets she hit didn't count.

Point out the cheater

At the 1976 Summer Olympics in Montreal, Boris Onischenko was on the Soviet Union's pentathlon team. Remember, there are five events in a pentathlon: horseback riding (show jumping), fencing, rifle shooting, swimming, and running.

Boris had won the silver medal four years earlier in Munich. His fencing score in 1972 was the best of any pentathlete. Now we may know why. In fencing, the equipment is electronically rigged, so that when your sword touches your opponent, a light goes on. That's how you score points. In 1976, while he was fencing against a British competitor, his opponent noticed that Boris was scoring points without touching him with his sword. They investigated and it turns out he had some kind of button in his hand that he would push and it would make the light go on! Yes, he was cheating, and yes, he was immediately disqualified.

For the birds

At the opening ceremony in Seoul, South Korea, in 1988, they released birds into the air. Many of them came to roost on the cauldron where the Olympic flame was about to be lit. When the moment came to light the cauldron, to signify the opening of the games, many of the birds got fried by the flame. After that they decided not to release birds into the air until *after* the lighting of the cauldron. At least no *humans* got hurt!

Technical difficulties

At the opening ceremony in Sydney, Australia, in 2000, the dramatic moment had come. They were about to light the Olympic flame, and the games would be officially under way. The person lighting the flame that day was Cathy Freeman, who went on to win the gold medal in the 400-meter track race. At the ceremony, they had an elaborate contraption to light the cauldron. First, Cathy lit the flame in a pool of water, and then the flame was to be lifted slowly up into the air until it reached the cauldron. One complication: it got stuck in midair. The stadium was filled, the world was watching, the dramatic music was playing, and nothing happened. It took several minutes until they got it going. What happened? They really don't know. When in doubt, blame it on a "computer glitch." Which is exactly what they did.

One of the all-time worst

Eddie Edwards made the British Olympic ski jumping team in 1988 and headed to Calgary to

compete in the Olympics. He was the first ever to represent Britain in ski jumping at a Winter Olympics. There was one slight problem: he was a terrible ski jumper. Maybe the worst in Olympic history. How did he make the team? He just applied. Nobody else did. He had trained in Australia and had recorded a so-so jump. So he was in. He proceeded to finish dead last in both the 70- and 90-meter jumps. Fans loved him. They identified with a regular guy who somehow made it to the Olympics. He got the nickname Eddie the Eagle. However, Olympic officials were not amused. They passed a rule that grounded all future "eagles."

The kneed to succeed

At the 1976 Summer Olympics in Montreal, the Soviet Union and Japan were engaged in an amazing battle for the gold medal in the men's team gymnastics event. Then tragedy struck the Japanese. Shun Fujimoto broke his right kneecap during the floor exercise. He was in terrible pain. But he didn't tell anyone. The competition was so close he felt he had to go on, which he did. He performed nearly flawlessly on the rings. He concluded his routine with a very difficult ending. He nailed a terrific landing with a broken kneecap. Nobody knew. He scored a marvelous 9.7 out of 10 and helped the Japanese win the gold medal!

Now that's a sportsman!

At the 1988 Summer Games in Seoul, South Korea, a sailor from Canada by the name of Lawrence Lemieux was all set to cross the finish line in second place and claim the silver medal. But he noticed that a sailor from Singapore had fallen out of his boat and was struggling in the water. Lemieux abandoned his race and saved his fellow sailor. Lemieux didn't win a sailing medal, but at the closing ceremony he was given a special medal for sportsmanship!

Treasure chest

The record for winning gold medals in one Olympics is held by Mark Spitz. At the 1972 Summer Games in Munich, the American swimmer won an amazing seven gold medals.

Ouch!

At the 1900 Olympics in Paris, one of the events was live pigeon shooting! A shooter from Belgium named Leon de Lunden was the winner. He killed twenty-one out of twenty-five birds, beating out a Frenchman by one. The event turned out to be quite messy and it was never held again. It was the one and only time that animals were killed in the name of sport at the Olympics.

There have been other sports that have come and gone at the Olympics. Between 1900 and 1920, for example, tug-of-war was an Olympic sport. Teams of eight competed. At the 1904 Olympics in St. Louis, only six teams entered, four from the U.S. and one each from Greece and South Africa. The rules permitted countries to enter more than one team. The U.S. swept the medals. In fact, the teams that finished first through fourth were all from the U.S.

Wrestlemania

If you wanted to get your money's worth, you would have gone to the wrestling matches at the

1912 Summer Olympics in Stockholm. Two matches stood out. I mean, really stood out. The light heavyweight final between Anders Ahlgren of Sweden and Ivar Bohling of Finland wouldn't end. It went on for nine hours. Since neither could figure out a way to win it, officials stopped the match and awarded each wrestler a silver medal. But the two of them were outdone in the same Olympics in a Greco-Roman wrestling match. It was a semifinal between another Finnish wrestler, Alfred Asikainen, and a Russian named Martin Klein. This match lasted eleven hours! Klein eventually won, but he was too exhausted to wrestle in the championship, so he went home with the silver medal.

You gotta be in it to win it

Did you hear the one about the guy who won the silver medal and didn't even show up? His name was Myer Prinstein, a Syracuse University long jumper. He competed in the 1900 Summer Olympics in Paris. He was a religious man, and since the finals were being held on a Sunday, he declined to participate on his Sabbath. But it didn't stop a fellow American named Alvin Kraenzlein from competing. Kraenzlein beat out Prinstein by one centimeter and claimed the gold medal. At that time qualifying jumps counted, so Prinstein went home with the silver medal. Was he happy with his prize? Not exactly. He was so angry at Kraenzlein that he went over to him and punched him in the face. So much for Olympic spirit!

The greatest record of all time

You've probably heard the phrase "records are made to be broken." In the Olympics you can do it by an inch or a hundredth of a second. Breaking a record is one thing, but smashing it to smithereens is something else. That's what twenty-two-year-old New Yorker Bob Beamon did at the 1968 Summer Olympics in Mexico City. He was a long jumper who barely qualified for the finals. But once he did, he made the most of it. The world record at the time in the long jump was 27 feet, $4\frac{3}{4}$ inches. Nobody had ever jumped more than 28 feet, ever. Bob Beamon didn't jump 28 feet either that day. He jumped more than 29 feet! Astounding. He broke the record by nearly two feet! He couldn't believe it, collapsing to the ground. His amazing record stood for another twenty-three years!

The wackiest race of all time

I'm not sure you can accurately call any particular race the "wackiest of all time," but let me submit the 1904 Olympic Marathon in St. Louis as a candidate.

The first man to cross the finish line was Fred Lorz, from New York. They placed a wreath on his head. But he didn't win! It turns out he was spotted riding in a car for a portion of the race when he wasn't feeling very well. When he felt better, he got out and ran the rest of the way. He said he just did it as a joke. Officials weren't laughing. They immediately banned him from racing. (They lifted the ban the next year, and he won the Boston Marathon without cheating.) The second man to cross the finish line in the 1904 Olympic Marathon was Thomas Hicks, another American from Massachusetts. He broke several of today's rules as well. During the race he took strychnine to keep him going. It worked like a stimulant. And he

was in such a bad state that he had to be helped across the finish line. All of this was apparently okay back then, and he was declared the winner of the race. Then there was a Cuban named Felix Carvajal. He ran in street clothes! He got so hungry during the race that he stopped to eat at an apple orchard. He wasn't feeling too great either, so he stopped to rest. And he still finished in fourth place! And to top it off, Len Taunyane from Africa finished ninth. That despite having to run off track by a considerable distance because he was being chased by a dog. If you know of a crazier race than this one, I'd love to hear about it.

OLYMPIC OVERTIME

You've heard the term "perfect 10." People use it all the time to refer to lots of stuff. Here's where it comes from: gymnastics. Athletes are awarded points for their routines, with the top score being a 10. Before 1976 at the Summer Games in Montreal, no athlete had ever received a 10. Then along came Nadia Comaneci of Romania. Just fourteen years old, she was four feet eleven inches tall, eighty-six pounds. On the uneven parallel bars she put on a dazzling performance, earning a perfect 10 from the judges. And she didn't stop there. Before the 1976 Olympic gymnastics competition was complete, she had earned six more perfect 10s!

The first American to score a perfect 10 in gymnastics was Mitch Gaylord, in 1984 in Los Angeles. He did it on the parallel bars. Moments later his teammate Peter Vidmar also scored a perfect 10 on the pommel horse.

There are five rings on the Olympic Flag, and they are blue, yellow, black, green, and red. Do you know why? There is one ring for each of the five parts of the world that joined the Olympic movement: Africa, the Americas, Asia, Australia, and Europe.

In July 1992 at the Summer Olympics in Barcelona, German diver Albin Killat jumped off the diving board, completed three somersaults, and then went kerplop. A belly flop of Olympic proportions. Needless to say, he didn't win a medal.

Justin Dumais competed for the U.S. in the 2004 Olympics in Athens. He didn't win a medal. He said his most embarrassing moment had occurred ten years earlier when he was sixteen. He was diving in a competition when his bathing suit came off. What to do? He first had to come up for air, and then he dove down to retrieve his Speedo suit!

EXTRA POINTS

So this brings us to one of the wackiest collections of stories you'll ever read. These are the stories that aren't exactly baseball or basketball or football, so I've lumped them all together into their own category. For example, ever hear of a boxing match that wound up underwater? What happens when a dog runs during a horse race? It's happened on purpose and by accident.

I've seen a horse race messed up by seagulls and even an earthquake. What happens when a jockey doesn't whip his horse, but decides to whip the jockey riding next to him? Animals are involved in all kinds of goofy situations, such as the Australian man who trains his mice to surf in his bathtub. Honest.

And world championships? They've got them in everything from toe wrestling to eating. And people try to set all kinds of records, like pulling stuff with their ears. Okay, you're right. This sounds really bizarre. But it's all true. So, read on. The best part is, you can't make this stuff up!

A little accident

In May 2004, some marketing "genius" decided to promote a jewelry company by implanting a flawless diamond into the nose of a race car. The diamond was worth $322,000. So they did it at the Monaco Grand Prix auto race. And you guessed it: the car had a minor accident and nobody could find the diamond. They say that "diamonds are forever." But I bet the job of that marketing executive wasn't!

'Tis the season

In December 2003, they had a nice fan promotion at the hockey game at Nassau Coliseum. The New York Islanders were hosting their bitter rivals, the New York Rangers. Since it was the Christmas season, the first 1,000 fans who came dressed up as Santa Claus got into the game free. And between periods of the game, they invited all of the Santas onto the ice. It was going well until one of the Santas took off his red coat to reveal that he was wearing a Rangers jersey. Several of the "Islander Santas" then started a hockey fight with the Rangers fan. What a lovely example of "peace on earth, goodwill toward men."

Not so lyrical

Then there is the saga of Caroline Marcil, an anthem singer in Quebec. It was April 2005, and she was called upon to sing "The Star-Spangled Banner" before a hockey exhibition game between the U.S. and Canada. She got out the "Oh, say, can you see" part okay, but shortly after that she sang a line that sounded like "what so twiley." Those words aren't in the national anthem, so she just stopped singing. As the crowd booed, she turned around and walked briskly off the ice to get the words. A few seconds later she returned with the lyrics in hand. She was now confident she could sing the national anthem without messing up. As she stepped back onto the ice, she slipped and fell hard, right on her rear end. It was more than just her ego that got bruised that night.

Tidal wave

In 1887, bare-knuckle boxing (without gloves) was illegal in the United States, but that didn't stop people from doing it. So here's what they did

one time for a championship fight. A tugboat left New York City at night with the boxers and spectators, and they came ashore on a beach on Long Island to stage the fight at sunrise. The fight was between Jack Dempsey (no relation to a more famous Jack Dempsey who was a heavyweight champ with gloves in the 1920s) and Johnny Reagan. During the eighth round, the tide came in and flooded the ring! So all the boxers and fans had to get back on the tugboat and find a dry spot to continue the fight, which they did. Eventually Dempsey won after forty-five rounds, and one long "tide delay."

Bell ringer

There was a much shorter and much more legal boxing match in Wheeling, West Virginia, in July 2003. Heavyweights James North and George Klinesmith were mixing it up, when Klinesmith went on the offensive in the fourth round. He knocked down North a couple times. The three-knockdown rule was in effect. So if he knocked him down a third time, the fight was over. In the final seconds of the round, North literally ran away from Klinesmith and jumped up onto the ropes to avoid the onslaught. He was hoping to be "saved by the bell." Klinesmith would have none of it. He raced over to North and landed a huge blow, knocking him backward, up and over the ropes, and completely out of the ring. Neither the bell nor the ropes could save North. Klinesmith was the winner!

No time to rest

In Atlantic City in February 2004, there was a controversial boxing match. Larry Marks was fighting Tokunbo Olajide in a junior middleweight championship fight. In the second round, Olajide was on the attack and he knocked Marks down. In boxing you have until the count of ten to prove to the referee that you are able to continue. Marks got up and was ready to go by the count of eight, but because he had two extra seconds to rest, he knelt down to catch his breath. Bad idea. The referee immediately ended the fight and declared Olajide the winner. The referee took the kneeling action to mean that Marks was unable to continue the fight.

Between the ropes

You expect lots of action inside the ring during a boxing match, but some unusual things happen when Floyd Mayweather Jr. fights. In a boxing match in January 2005, by the seventh round of Mayweather's fight with Henry Bruseles, Mayweather was winning easily. During the middle of the action, one of the TV announcers calling the fight turned to the other and asked on the air: "Do you like the Steelers or the Patriots?" The two football teams were due to meet the next day in the AFC Championship game. Well, I guess Mayweather was pretty bored with the fight as well, because, as he was fighting, he turned toward the announcers and yelled out, "The Patriots!" Turns out Mayweather could predict football games as well as he could box. He won his fight in the next round, and the Patriots went on to win the next day as well.

It got a little crazier for Mayweather in April 2006. He was fighting Zab Judah in Las Vegas for the International Boxing Federation welterweight title. In the tenth round, Judah hit Mayweather with two illegal punches: 1) a low blow below the belt and 2) a punch to the back of the head.

Mayweather's corner was angry. His trainer charged into the ring to attack Judah. Judah's trainer then jumped into the ring to go after Mayweather's trainer. All sorts of people started running into the ring to fight. Fans started throwing food. Police had to be called to quiet down what was turning into a riot. Again Mayweather won, and again, a Mayweather fight produced something rather unusual.

The bare truth

In September 2003 at a track meet in Frankfurt, Germany, German pole vaulter Tim Lobinger was quite excited that he won the pole vault that day by soaring 19 feet 4¾ inches. In his exuberance, he ran a victory lap and pulled down his shorts, exposing his rear end. He was doing it to protest some of the earlier judging in the event. He said he thought it was "funny." Track and field officials failed to see the humor. They fined him $5,000 for "unbecoming behavior."

One little problem

In 1966, a rugby match was about to start in Wales between Colwyn Bay and Portmadoc. The teams lined up and were all set to go, but the game had to be called off. They forgot to bring a ball.

Like cats and dogs

In February 2004, there were too many animals on the racetrack. It happened at Aqueduct Raceway in New York. Right in the middle of the horse race, a dog decided to run for his life. The horses were galloping toward the finish line, and the dog darted out and ran across the track right in front of the hard-charging horses. He made it safely to the other side of the track. It's interesting to note that one of the horses in the race was named "King of the Cats." I'm happy to report that nobody "fought like cats and dogs," and nobody got hurt!

Like horses and dogs

One time there was a dog on the racetrack on purpose. In June 2004 at Kempton Park in London, there was a special match race staged. It was a race between a horse and a dog. The horse, named Tiny Tim, would go head-to-head against a greyhound named Simply Fabulous. Which one do you think won? The oddsmakers made the horse the heavy favorite. And they were wrong! The dog easily won the race. The horse's fans said they made the race too short (400 meters). If it were longer, the horse probably would have won it over the long haul.

They switch horses, don't they?

At least that race was on the level. In 1982, at another English racetrack, Leicester Racecourse, there was a race for two-year-old horses. A horse by the name of Flockton Grey won by an astounding twenty lengths. Everyone was amazed. How could the horse win by such a large margin? There was an easy explanation. The horse wasn't really Flockton Grey. The owner and trainer had cooked up a little scheme to make a lot of money. They switched Flockton Grey with a three-year-old horse named Good Hand, and went about betting on the phony Flockton Grey to win. When Good Hand *handily* beat the younger horses, the owner and trainer won a ton of money—until the scam was figured out. They were fined and banned from horse racing.

Mother nature comes calling

So they were right in the middle of the second horse race at Hollywood Park in Los Angeles in

June 2005, when an earthquake hit. What did they do? They kept racing, of course. The track announcer Vic Stauffer didn't miss a beat. As he called out the names of the horses, he said, "We are in the midst of an earthquake in Southern California." As for the race, it was a photo finish between Pleasant Thunder and Dark Beauty. Stauffer jokingly announced that he didn't know who the winner was and he didn't care either, giving the impression that he was more concerned with his safety. (Dark Beauty turned out to be the winner by a nose.) For the record, the quake measured 4.9, which is considered mild by earthquake standards.

The attack of the seagulls

In March 2005, there were supposed to be twelve animals on the track for a horse race, but by the time the race was over, you couldn't tell how many were there, and what exactly was going on. It was the last race of the day at Sandown Raceway in Melbourne, Australia. As the horses rounded the final turn and headed for home, a flock of seagulls, too many to count, attacked the horses! Five

of the jockeys fell off their mounts. One of them broke his arm. It was mayhem. Horses, jockeys, seagulls, and feathers flying everywhere. The track announcer yelled out, "It's a complete debacle here." Race officials had no choice but to declare it "no race." Bettors were refunded their money. It was a horse race that was truly "for the birds"! And in this case, somebody *did* get hurt.

Give that man a hand

It was April 2005, and it was a close race at Aqueduct Raceway in New York. Two horses were charging to the finish line. Jose Santos was aboard Exaggerate, and Jean-Luc Samyn was the jockey on Dr. Rockett. The two horses were galloping side by side when suddenly Samyn started to fall off his horse. As he was scrambling to right himself, Santos reached over to help push him back into his saddle. Exaggerate won the race, and give Santos an extra round of applause for his "helping hand"!

The sportsmanship was not nearly so terrific in Bairnsdale, Australia, in January 2006. They were running the Bairnsdale Cup when two horses bumped during the race. Jockey Danny Adam wasn't happy. So right in the middle of the race, he reached over and punched fellow jockey Michael Guthrie in the face. Adam wasn't finished. A bit later on he took his whip, and instead of using it on his horse, he started swatting Guthrie with it. Neither jockey was a factor in the race. Adam finished fourth, Guthrie finished sixth. In fact, Adam wasn't a factor for some time to come. His unsportsmanlike conduct resulted in a four-month suspension.

World champion

How would you like to be a world champion? They seem to have championships in just about everything. I've seen the World Beard and Mustache Championships. (They stage it every other year. I think that's to give the contestants lots of time for their hair to grow.) How about the World Rock Paper Scissors Championships? They have that one in England. And since little kids are likely to kick other little kids in the shin, they made a championship out of that! That's in England, too. It's the World Shin Kicking Championships. Two guys hold each other and start kicking. The guy who is left standing wins. And it's not just for kids. In 2004 the winner was Joe McDonough. He was forty years old! He certainly had a lot of years to practice his shin kicking.

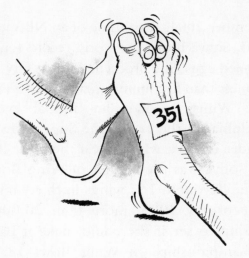

How about toe wrestling? Yup, toe wrestling. In England in July 2005, they held the annual Toe Wrestling Championships. Two competitors sit down and lock their feet together by their toes. The toe wrestler who forces his opponent's foot over "a line" is declared the winner. Anyway, Paul Beech, who is known as "the Toeminator," successfully defended his title. That is one wacky "toe-nament."

How about eating championships? Sonya Thomas is a lady from Virginia who is nicknamed the Black Widow. She is a world champion eater who often shows up at sports events. For example, in November 2004, at halftime of an NBA game in Orlando, Sonya broke the world record for eating hard-boiled eggs. She proceeded to eat fifty-two of them in less than five minutes. Yummy!

The Wing Bowl is an annual event in Philadelphia on the eve of the Super Bowl. The whole idea is to see who can eat the most chicken wings. Sonya was the winner of Wing Bowl 12, when she devoured 167 wings in thirty minutes. So in February 2005, more than 20,000 fans showed up to see if she could make it back-to-back championships in Wing Bowl 13. Well, after thirty minutes she had eaten 147 wings, the exact same number as Bill "El Wingador" Simmons. What to do? An eat-off! And in the two minutes of sudden death, El Wingador ate one more wing than the Black Widow. Simmons was the winner!

Undaunted, Sonya entered a bratwurst-eating contest the following August in Sheboygan, Wisconsin. She not only won, she obliterated the old record of nineteen sausages eaten in ten minutes. The Black Widow devoured thirty-five bratwursts! She is clearly the best when it comes to eating "wurst."

World records

In Dachau, Germany, in November 2005, all sorts of people gathered to try to set strange world records. And boy, were they strange. One strongman lifted weights with his ears! He attached string to his ears and picked up weights. You really need strong string, not to mention strong ears, to do that. Another lady was Shobha Tipnis from India. Her specialty was having strong lungs. She blew up a hot water bottle until it burst. But my personal favorite was a guy named Eckhard Schroeder. His record? Sitting silently and smiling for seven straight hours. Talk about talent. Some people are great golfers like Tiger Woods. Others are great basketball players, like Lebron James. But Eckhard Schroeder is the world's best sitter-and-smiler-all-at-once. I'm wondering, if you stand and smile, or sit and frown, are those two different records?

Look, Mom, no hands

In the former Soviet republic of Georgia, Lasha Pataridze is another guy with strong ears. In November 2003, he attached strings to his ears

and tied the strings to a delivery van. He then proceeded to pull the van down the street. In April
2006, he pulled two trucks that weighed four and
a half tons for forty yards, all with his ears. The
trucks were tied together, and they in turn were
tied to his ears! He sets world records by possess-
ing the world's strongest ears. The records may

never be broken, because when you think about it, who would really want to break them?

Another record setter is New Yorker Ashrita Furman. Nobody has set more Guinness World Records. All kinds of stuff, from juggling to balancing milk cartons on his chin to climbing mountains on a pogo stick. Well, in January 2006, he went underwater with scuba gear to set another record. He was in an aquarium in Malaysia, trying to break his record of juggling balls underwater. The record was forty-eight minutes and thirty-six seconds. He was doing just fine until a shark swam by and in effect said, "Not in my house." The shark interrupted the juggling, forcing Furman to start all over. On his second effort, he was so exhausted he quit after about thirty-seven minutes. By the way, reports out of Malaysia claimed the shark's name was Guinness!

Basic training

Don't ask why, but a man in Australia has three pet mice. Their names are Chopsticks, Harry, and Bunsen. He is training them to surf! He has built little surfboards, and he trains the mice in his

bathtub. Then he takes them to the ocean, finds a small wave, and off they go. So the next time you see a surfer "hanging 10" (surfing at the front of the board so that all ten toes are hanging off), it might be a mouse! Then again, a mouse has only four toes on his front feet. So if he's standing on those feet, he might be "hanging 8"!

Happy ending

In March 2006 in the Italian Alps, there was a skiing competition. As Jani Pogacar of Slovenia was skiing down the mountain, an avalanche struck. Snow completely engulfed him. But Jani kept skiing, and he made it out alive. He was totally fine. Jani is the very embodiment of my favorite saying: "And nobody got hurt!"

THE RECAP

So, there you have it. Baseball players who didn't use their gloves, and some who did when they shouldn't have. Balls taking all sorts of bounces, even off shortstops' heads. And a golfer who even conked himself on the head with his own golf club. You had the soccer fan who "scored himself," not the ball. Not real smart since the authorities were chasing him. And you saw how showboating isn't real bright in either football or snowboard cross. And if you ever win a prize in sports, please make every effort to hold on to it, unlike the Olympian who tossed his gold medal into the lake by mistake. In summary, all kinds of goofy stuff continues to happen. And that's a good thing. Maybe not for the person who goofed up, but for you and me. I get to write about it, and you get to read it. So I'll make you the same deal I made last time.

The Recap

You keep enjoying sports, and I'll keep collecting wild and crazy sports stories. Hopefully we'll talk again down the road. And when we share our outrageous sports stories, let's hope that once again we can all say, "AND NOBODY GOT HURT!"

Emmy Award–winning sportscaster LEN BERMAN has been collecting weird and wacky sports stories to show on his TV segment "Spanning the World" for more than twenty years. A regular on NBC's *Today Show*, Len is a six-time winner of the Sportscaster of the Year Award given by the National Sportscasters and Sportswriters Association, and he has reported on major sports events around the globe, including multiple Olympic Games.

KENT GAMBLE has been a freelance illustrator since 1977. His work has appeared in the *New York Times, People, Golf Digest, Marvel Comics,* and many other periodicals. He has illustrated three humorous books published by Texas Tech University Press, as well as the children's book *Look Who's Going to Texas Tech,* by Marsha Gustafson. He lives in Lubbock, Texas.

The HOME RUN KID is back!

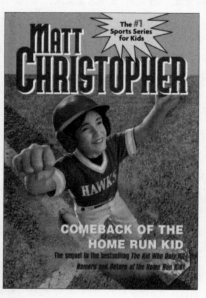

Sylvester Coddmyer III, star of *The Kid Who Only Hit Homers* and *Return of the Home Run Kid,* is about to face his biggest challenge yet. His second season with the Hooper Redbirds is over and he's looking forward to the start of summer baseball, when he sprains his left ankle in a freak accident. How will he hit homers when every swing means pain?

And look for these other Home Run Kid titles, too!

Available wherever books are sold.
www.lb-kids.com • www.mattchristopher.com